SEARCH FOR STEAM

British Rail 1963–1966

CHARLIE VERRALL

AMBERLEY

First published 2019

Amberley Publishing
The Hill, Stroud
Gloucestershire, GL5 4EP

www.amberley-books.com

British Library Cataloguing in Publication Data.
A catalogue record for this book is available from the British Library.

ISBN 978 1 4456 8535 9 (print)
ISBN 978 1 4456 8536 6 (ebook)

Typeset in 10pt on 12pt Sabon.
Origination by Amberley Publishing.
Printed in the UK.

Contents

Introduction

I started taking photographs of British Railways steam locomotives and steam-hauled trains from as early as 1950, and continued to do so almost until the end of steam. In the early days I had the advantage of being from a railway family: my grandfather had retired as a driver at New Cross Gate, an uncle was a driver at Norwood and my father was a booking office clerk. In fact, after leaving school in 1953, I too joined the Southern Region and remained in railway employment until 1967.

From 1948 I travelled to school on a daily basis from Wivelsfield to Hove, passing both the works and engine sheds at Brighton. After joining the Southern Region I was based in the offices at both Redhill and East Croydon and, armed with a number of lineside passes, continued to take photographs. These photographs were taken in most of the regions of British Railways. Most of those prior to the end of 1962 are contained in two earlier publications.

The intention of this book is to cover the period from 1963 to 1966. In 1967, most of the steam workings were in the North West of England and sadly it was not practical for me to visit those locations at weekends, in the main because I was working in London. This is, in essence, a photographic diary of places visited and sights seen. All my logs were lost many years ago.

Chapter One

1963 – A Mixed Photographic Year

In the early months of 1963 I took very few photographs. Firstly, there was the worst period of snow for many years; secondly, I had some family matters that needed my attention; and lastly, I had become disillusioned following the withdrawal of so many locomotives in December 1962, primarily for accountancy purposes, including a number which I had photographed just months before, including several A4 Pacifics and all of the ex-LBCR K Class 2-6-0s.

It was not until 2 February that I was to take any photographs. On that day I visited Redhill where, in the snow, Schools Class No. 30930 *Radley* and U1s Nos 31900 and 31903 were at the back of the shed, awaiting their fates. All three had been withdrawn at the end of December 1962, and would eventually be towed to Eastleigh and broken up, although in the case of No. 30930, this was not until April 1964. Later on the same day

U1 Class Nos 31900 and 31903 and Schools Class No. 30930 *Radley* at Redhill shed. 2 February 1963.

a visit was made to Wood Green, where in the previous two years I had taken a number of photographs of A3s and A4s in particular. Deltic D9008, later to be named *The Green Howards,* worked the 9.40 Newcastle to King's Cross and A1 No. 60158 *Aberdonian* the 14.10 King's Cross to York. This was to prove to be my last visit to that area.

Moving back to the family home next to Wivelsfield station gave a few opportunities for lineside photography. One such opportunity was on 3 March when West Country Class No. 34019 *Bideford* worked the 14.38 empty vans from Brighton to New Cross Gate, more than likely to form part of one of the following day's Down newspaper trains. At the time Brighton had several Bullied Light Pacific diagrams, including the two Down newspaper trains, through services to Plymouth and Cardiff via Salisbury (prior to the 1962 winter timetable there had also been a through service to Bournemouth West via Southampton), and Up freights to Norwood and Bricklayers Arms from Brighton and Newhaven. Living at the foot of the embankment, we were well aware of the arrival of the last two when, climbing the ruling incline, the house shook. On 31 March the Bluebell Railway Preservation Society ran a special train from Victoria to Sheffield Park via Haywards Heath and Horsted Keynes, 'The Spring Belle'. Between Victoria and Haywards Heath, Standard 4MTT No. 80084 double-headed E4 Class 473 *Birch Grove.* No. 80084 was detached at Haywards Heath and sent light engine to Brighton for turning before heading the return journey to Victoria. *Birch Grove* remained at the rear as Adams Tank No. 488 headed the train to Horsted Keynes. On the return, Nos 473 and 488 worked as far as Haywards Heath.

Just a single photograph was taken in April, when on the 27th rebuilt Battle of Britain Class No. 34089 *602 Squadron* was on Brighton shed. A Brighton engine at the time, No. 34089 had the doubtful privilege on 3 October 1966 of being the last steam locomotive to be outshopped from Eastleigh Works in BR days.

A1 Class No. 60158 *Aberdonian* near Wood Green with the 14.10 King's Cross to York. 2 February 1963.

West Country Class No. 34019 *Bideford* leaving Wivelsfield with the 14.38 vans from Brighton to New Cross Gate. 3 March 1963.

BR Standard 4MTT No. 80084 and E4 Class No. 473 *Birch Grove* between Copyhold Junction and Haywards Heath with 'The Spring Belle' special from Victoria to Sheffield Park. 31 March 1963.

0415 Class No. 488 leaving Haywards Heath with 'The Spring Belle' special to Sheffield Park. E4 Class No. 473 *Birch Grove* is at the rear. 31 March 1963.

Rebuilt Battle of Britain Class No. 34089 *602 Squadron* at Brighton shed. 27 April 1963.

On 11 May another photographic visit was made to Brighton, producing just two images, both of which are of interest. Firstly, No. 34019 *Bideford* again, this time seen looking down from the top of the cliff face at Howard Place. To protect unwary spotters there was a high flint wall; otherwise, the possibility of a fatal fall would have resulted. When spotting as schoolboys we used to go further toward New England Road, where a good view of what was on shed could be seen, as typified in several photographs taken by Howard Bennett in the late 1890s/early 1900s. The other photograph was taken from Platforms 1 and 2 at Brighton station of USA tank DS236, the former No. 30074, fresh from repainting at Eastleigh and on its way to become one of the Lancing Carriage Works shunters.

One of the advantages of working the Engine Diagrams section at East Croydon was that, being next to the Motive Power section, we would get notification of withdrawals as they were announced. One such prior notice led me to go to Brighton Shed on 1 June to see E4 Class No. 32479 on its last day in service – being the last LBSCR locomotive working from Brighton. Also seen was Schools Class No. 30911 *Dover*, which had been towed from the dump of withdrawn locomotives at Hove, and which was being readied for its last journey to Eastleigh for scrapping. No. 30911 was the last Schools to work on the Central Section when, on 28 December, it worked the 07.27 Reading to London Bridge. Instead of returning to Reading, it then worked the 16.40 to Brighton, and the next day it was sent to join four other Schools Class locomotives in the storage dump in Hove Goods Yard. Also on shed was Class 2MTT No. 41312, one of the last steam

West Country Class No. 34019 *Bideford* on Brighton shed, as viewed from Howard Place. The buildings of Brighton Works can be seen in the background. 11 May 1963.

USA Class DS236 at Brighton shed prior to commencing duties at Lancing Carriage Works. 11 May 1963.

locomotives to work on the Steyning line, and later to pass into preservation. Later I was to go to Redhill and photographed two of the resident N Class 2-6-0s, Nos 31850 and 31852. No. 31850 was to be withdrawn during the following January but was found not to be moveable and was scrapped where it stood. Seen taking coal was U Class No. 31797.

Stored awaiting disposal was the withdrawn N1 Class No. 31876. Back to the lineside at Wivelsfield on 27 July, Battle of Britain No. 34057 *Biggin Hill* was seen working the 10.57 Walsall to Hastings via Lewes. Further inter-regional services were seen from the footbridge at Gatwick Airport on 10 August: Standard 4 4-6-0 No. 75068 on the 10.45 Hastings to Walsall; N Class No. 31873 on the 11.39 Eastbourne to Leicester; and N Class No. 31833 on the 12.01 Eastbourne to Stoke. Redhill shed was one place I was to visit several times in 1963: on 20 September N Class No. 31410 was seen receiving attention before working a service more than likely to Reading, and another N Class, the withdrawn No. 31825, was stored at the rear of the shed.

There were several other photographers working in the offices at East Croydon, one of whom was Malcolm Burton, the Chairman of the Locomotive Club of Great Britain. He suggested to me that I should get fully back into taking railway photographs and as a result I went on a LCGB visit to Swindon on 22 December. As expected there were a number of withdrawn locomotives there, awaiting their destiny. Included were 57xx Class Nos 3653, 4690 (acting as shed/works pilot), 6724 and 9604; 94xx Class No. 8461, 45xx Class No. 4507; 56xx Class No. 6618; Hall Class No. 5943 *Elmdon Hall*; Grange Class No. 6814 *Enborne Grange*; King Class Nos 6011 *King James I* and 6025 *King Henry III*, and many more locos which I did not photograph. As well as No. 4690, in steam was Hall Class No. 5955 *Garth Hall*. Also of note was railcar W21W, bearing the legend 'COND'.

E4 Class No. 32479 at Brighton Shed. 1 June 1963.

Schools Class No. 30911 *Dover* at Brighton Shed after being brought back from Hove dump. In the background can be seen the cliff face leading up to Howard Place. 1 June 1963.

N Class No. 31850 at Redhill shed. 1 June 1963.

U Class No. 31797 being coaled at Redhill. 1 June 1963.

Battle of Britain Class No. 34057 *Biggin Hill* leaving Wivelsfield with the 10.57 Walsall to Hastings.
27 July 1963.

N Class No. 31833 approaching Gatwick Airport with 12.01 Eastbourne to Stoke. Note the Bristol
Britannia in the background. 8 August 1963.

N Class No. 31410, with extensions to the smoke deflector plates, at Redhill shed. 20 September 1963.

Withdrawn 57xx Class No. 4690 acting as shed pilot, Swindon. December 22 1963.

Grange Class No. 6814 *Enborne Grange* withdrawn at Swindon. 22 December 1963.

King Class No. 6011 *King James I* partly dismantled at Swindon. 22 December 1963.

King Class No. 6025 *King Henry III* withdrawn at Swindon. 22 December 1963.

Diesel railcar W21W awaiting scrapping at Swindon. 22 December 1963.

Hall Class No. 5955 *Garth Hall* in steam at Swindon. 22 December 1963.

Chapter Two

1964 – A Much More Productive Year

Following on from the successful photographic visit to Swindon, on 25 January I made a visit to Eastleigh. Stored within the shed were at least six Brighton Terriers, all of which were to be bought for preservation, the last two B4 0-4-0 tanks, No. 30586 (the only Beattie tank to be broken up) and at least two Schools Class 4-4-0s, including No. 30903 *Charterhouse*. I managed to photograph some twenty-one of the withdrawn locos which were lined up awaiting scrapping. These included H Class No. 31543; Ns Nos 31409, 31857, 31865 and 31871; M7s Nos 30125 and 30055; Z Class No. 30951; Q1 Class No. 33025; Ws Nos 31911, 31913 and 31920; un-rebuilt Light Pacifics Nos 34011 *Tavistock*, 34049 *Anti-Aircraft Command* and 34069 *Hawkinge*; Us Nos 31622 and 31808; 700 Class 0-6-s Nos 30697 and 30700; and LMS 'Mickey Mouse' Class 2 tanks Nos 41292, 41297, 41306 and 41308. There were many more besides. The good news was that photographs were also taken of six operational Light Pacifics, two USA tanks and Class 9 No. 92215.

As a general rule I was not interested in railtours, neither from a photographic point of view nor travelling on them. However, there are always exceptions to the rule. On 22 March the RCTS and LCGB jointly ran 'The Sussex Downsman' railtour, part of which ran from Tunbridge Wells West to Polegate via the Cuckoo Line and on to Pevensey. This portion of the tour was hauled by Battle of Britain Class No. 34066 *Spitfire*, the locomotive involved in the serious accident at St Johns in December 1957. Strangely, an uncle of mine was a member of the London Fire Brigade and was called out to attend this incident. I wonder if No. 34066 was specifically requested for the special working since it was the first Bullied Pacific to visit Heathfield in July 1955. After working the railtour as far as Pevensey, No. 34066 ran light engine to Brighton, prior to working the return special to Victoria via Uckfield. I happened to be on the platform at Brighton when No. 34066 arrived and the fireman, a friend of mine of several years, invited me onto the footplate. He said that they were going to turn the loco and asked whether I'd like to join them. I assumed we were going to use the turntable in Brighton shed, but instead we proceeded to Brighton Top Yard and used the turntable there opposite Montpelier Junction. I suspect not many non-footplatemen made that particular journey!

My next BR photographic trip was not until 5 April, when I joined a LCGB party on a trip to Swindon, Barrow Road and St Philip's Marsh. At Swindon there was a collection of recently withdrawn locos including County Class No. 1014 *County of Glamorgan*, Jinty No. 47557 and 9400 Class 9425. King Class 6023 *King Henry III* appeared not to

H Class No. 31543 waiting to be scrapped at Eastleigh. 25 January 1964.

U Class No. 31622 waiting to be scrapped at Eastleigh. 25 January 1964.

West Country No. 34011 *Tavistock* waiting to be scrapped at Eastleigh. 25 January 1964.

USA Class No. 30073 at Eastleigh. 25 January 1964.

Class 9 No. 92215 at Eastleigh. 25 January 1964.

have moved from the position I saw it at in December. 4575 Class No. 5568, withdrawn in January 1963, was present and was not broken up until June. Recently out of the paintshop were Modified Hall No. 6967 *Willesley Hall* and 4200 Class No. 5202. At Barrow Road the shortly to be withdrawn Jubilee Class No. 45682 *Trafalgar* was in steam, as were 4Fs Nos 44264, 44269 and 44534. 9F No. 92248 was also darkening the skies. Finally at St Philip's Marsh Britannia No. 70018 *Flying Dutchman* was present as well as Castle No. 7014 *Caerhays Castle*, Hall No. 5934 *Kneller Hall* and Modified Hall No. 6999 *Capel Dewi Hall*. No. 5934 was to be withdrawn the following month.

On 24 April I was in Northumberland visiting some industrial sites but managed to take a photograph of Q6 No. 63413 working coal empties through Newsham. Visits to industrial sites and taking photographs became a feature of my life from then on. The following day, 25 April, I had retained our hire car and went to the large NCB sheds and workshops at Philadelphia, and in miserable weather took the chance to see some of the trip workings at Fencehouses and Penshaw; those that I saw were worked by Q6 No. 63384 and No. 63453, although Class 2 Bo-Bo diesel D5168 was also seen, complete with a braking tender between it and the train of loaded wagons.

In 1961 and 1962 I was to visit Basingstoke several times and returned for a final time on 16 May. By then all the West of England services were being hauled by Warship Class diesels and the only steam workings were those to Bournemouth and Weymouth; in addition the former Somerset and Dorset inter-regional trains were now routed via Basingstoke. One of these was the 10.00 Bournemouth to York, the 'Pines Express', hauled by unrebuilt West Country Class No. 34102 *Lapford* – one of the last to remain in service.

Jinty No. 47557 at Swindon, waiting to be broken up. 5 April 1964.

4575 Class No. 5568 at Swindon after withdrawal. 5 April 1964.

Modified Hall No. 6967 *Willesley Hall* at Swindon ex paint shop. 5 April 1964.

4200 Class No. 5202, from the Swindon paint shop. 5 April 1964.

Jubilee No. 45682 *Trafalgar* at Barrow Road. 5 April 1964.

Class 9 No. 92248 at Barrow Road. 5 April 1964.

Barrow Road shed yard. 5 April 1964.

Britannia No. 70018 *Flying Dutchman* at St Philip's Marsh. 5 April 1964.

Modified Hall No. 6999 *Capel Dewi Hall* at St Philip's Marsh. 5 April 1964.

Q6 Class No. 63453 at Fencehouses with a local trip working. 25 April 1964.

Station buildings at Fencehouses. 25 April 1964.

Q6 Class No. 63453 on a local trip working at Penshaw. 25 April 1964.

My final photographs taken in May, on the 31st, were firstly of LMS Class 5 No. 45349 north of Clayton Tunnel heading a special train from Northampton to Brighton. During my period in the Engine Diagrams section at Essex House it was frequently the practice for 'foreign' locomotives to work through, especially if the timings did not allow for an engine change en route. The other photograph taken on that day was earlier in the morning of electric locomotive No. 20001 passing through Wivelsfield on the 08.25 Victoria to Newhaven Marine boat train. The three Hornby locos regularly worked these services, supplemented at different times by LBSCR H2 Atlantics, King Arthurs and Schools Class engines, until replaced by electric multiple units. Although obviously not steam locomotives, they were particular favourites of mine. Why one of these important locomotives was not retained for preservation is to me a mystery, even more so the scrapping after a long period in storage of the five LMS and Southern main line diesels: Nos 10000, 10001, 10201, 10202 and 10203. A year or so after this image was taken I managed to get a pass to ride in the cab of a Hornby from Hove to London Bridge on a parcels train working. One thing I recall was how small the cab was. When the driver, inspector and myself were on board it was very cramped, and the secondman/fireman was forced to ride in the rear cab – not a pleasant ride.

As explained earlier, I did not as a rule follow and photograph railtours. However, I was out on 5 July, when the LCGB ran 'The Surrey Wanderer' railtour. This was a timings clerk's nightmare, going from Waterloo to Shepperton, then to Wimbledon, where a switch from South Western to Central Division lines was made, before going

West Country Class No. 34106 *Lapford* leaving Basingstoke with the 10.00 Bournemouth to York 'Pines Express'. 16 May 1964.

SR electric loco No. 20001 leaving Wivelsfield with the 08.25 Victoria to Newhaven Marine. 31 May 1964.

on to West Croydon via Beddington Lane, West Croydon to Epsom Downs and back, followed by West Croydon to Tulse Hill via Selhurst, Tulse Hill to Beckenham Junction and then via the little-used spur to Norwood Junction and Caterham. Then, back from Caterham to Purley and to Tattenham Corner, from Tattenham Corner via Crystal Palace and Clapham Junction to Kensington Olympia, and finally from Olympia to Victoria (Eastern). It is no wonder the various timetable offices developed an unofficial telegraph code for such workings as DAA: Daft as Ar----s! Two locomotives were used, Standard Class 2 2-6-0 No. 78038 and M7 Class No. 30053.

Back to normality on 11 July, when on a visit to WD Bicester, I photographed Grange Class 6849 *Walton Grange* at Oxford. On 17 July, on an industrial visit to some ironstone sites, a quick visit was made to Woodford Halse sheds where the long withdrawn J39/1 No. 64747 and V2 No. 60810 were seen. My final photographs for July were taken just north of Wivelsfield station. These were of LMS Class 5 No. 44938 on the 07.00 excursion from Coventry to Eastbourne and Standard 5 No. 73038 on an Up special working. Also seen was Crompton D6504 on the 10.05 Eastbourne to Accrington return special.

On 8 August a visit was made to Hatton, where several steam workings were seen. These included Modified Hall Class No. 6966 *Witchingham Hall* on the 10.10 Poole to Birkenhead, Modfied Hall No. 6991 *Acton Burnell Hall* with the 09.05 Birkenhead to Poole, Castle Class No. 7024 *Powis Castle* on the 10.24 Birkenhead to Ramsgate, Hall Class No. 6933 *Birtles Hall* with the 11.00 Wolverhampton to Weymouth, Grange Class No. 6871 *Bourton Grange* on the 13.11 Portsmouth to Wolverhampton and finally

M7 Class No. 30053 leaving Purley for Tattenham Corner with 'The Surrey Wanderer' railtour. 5 July 1964.

Grange Class No. 6849 *Walton Grange* at Oxford. 11 July 1964.

Class J39/1 No. 64747 stored at Woodford Halse. 17 July 1964.

V2 Class No. 60810 on the wheeldrop at Woodford Halse shed. 11 July 1964.

LMS Class 5 No. 44938 north of Wivelsfield with the 07.00 excursion Coventry to Eastbourne. 27 July 1964.

Hall Class No. 6937 *Conyngham Hall* on the 11.05 Weymouth to Wolverhampton. Additionally, Crompton D6518 worked the 10.27 Brighton to Wolverhampton. The empty stock from this train was worked back by fellow Crompton D6515, which had worked the 08.35 from Ramsgate. The following day, 9 July, I caught a local bus to just outside of Ardingly and climbed down the railway embankment to the eastern face of Lywood Tunnel, where Class E4473 *Birch Grove* was stabled while on loan to Demolition & Construction Limited to assist with the removal of the track from Lywood Tunnel to Horsted Keynes.

By 20 September I was in the Manchester area at the start of a photographic holiday. Armed with a number of shed permits, I had left Euston amid all the rebuilding works; my first visit was to Gorton, where several withdrawn engines were seen. These included B1 No. 61269, a December 1963 withdrawal, Crab No. 42902, withdrawn in March 1964, Jubilee No. 45578 *United Provinces* and 4F 0-6-0 No. 43856; in steam were Class 5 No. 45386, 8F No. 48129, Jinty No. 47306 and WDs Nos 90080 and 90402.

On the 21st I went to Longsight shed, by now almost devoid of a steam allocation but containing the withdrawn Crab No. 42842 and Royal Scot No. 46129 *The Scottish Horse*. In steam were 8Fs No. 48136 – although allocated to Newton Heath but devoid of a shed plate – and No. 48679, and Jubilee No. 45632 *Tonga* complete with the 'Not south of Crewe' stripes on the cab side; Class A Bo-Bo electric locomotive E3001 was also present. The 22nd proved to be a busy day, firstly visiting Patricroft where 8F No. 48129 was seen from the station footbridge passing the signal box. On shed were at least three Jinties – Nos 47365, 47378 *Black Magic* and 47616 *Nobby*, all names being painted on locally.

Modified Hall Class No. 6966 *Witchingham Hall* on Hatton bank with the 10.10 Poole to Birkenhead. 8 August 1964.

Modified Hall No. 6991 *Acton Burnell Hall* descending Hatton bank with the 09.05 Birkenhead to Poole. 8 August 1964.

E4 Class No. 473 *Birch Grove* and Ruston & Hornsby Class 48DS diesel shunter No. 269599 at Lywood, waiting to work on track removal duties. 5 August 1964.

Jubilee Class No. 45578 *United Provinces* stored at Gorton after withdrawal. 20 September 1964.

Jinty No. 47306 at Gorton.
20 September 1964.

WD 2-8-0 No. 90080 at Gorton. 20 September 1964.

Jubilee Class No. 45632 *Tonga* at Longsight. 21 September 1964.

Royal Scot Class No. 46129 *The Scottish Horse* stored at Longsight after withdrawal. 21 September 1964.

8F No. 48136 at Longsight. 21 September 1964.

Class A BoBo electric E3001 at Longsight. 21 September 1964.

Also in steam was Stanier Class 4 tank No. 42297. Only two locos were photographed at Rose Grove shed: the shortly to be withdrawn 4F No. 44468, complete with the 'Not south of Crewe' stripe, and 8F No. 48281. Continuing on to Bolton, not a lot was photographed. One of the former Horwich Works shunters, L&Y Class 23 No. 11305, was in a shed, as was withdrawn Fowler Dock Tank No. 47165; outside the shed was Standard 2 tank No. 84026 and Crab No. 42778. My next stop was Agecroft shed, where withdrawn Crab No. 42860 and Crab No. 42901 were in a photographical position. 23 September was not quite such a busy day, mainly comprising a visit to Newton Heath station and sheds. At the station double-chimney Caprotti Class 5 No. 44687 was seen working a freight train, whereas in the shed withdrawn Fowler Class 4 tank No. 42379 was present together with recently withdrawn Jubilee No. 45592 *Indore*. Also on shed was B1 No. 61010 *Wildebeeste*, 4F No. 44548 and Class 5 No. 44729. This concluded an interesting and productive visit to some of the sheds in the Manchester area, together with the sight of some of the remaining trolley buses and the Lancashire & Yorkshire Railway façade to Victoria station.

The following day, 24 September, I had crossed the Pennines and was at Barrow Hill shed to see, among others, 0F 0-4-0 saddle tank No. 47001 and Deeley 0-4-0 tank No. 41528, both of which were among the main line locos that worked at the local Staverley Steelworks; also on shed was WD 2-8-0 No. 90384. On my way further north, Jubilee Class No. 45597 *Barbados* was seen at Sheffield Midland waiting to depart with the 16.30 to Leeds. I was on my way to visit NCB sites in Northumberland and the only main line steam I recorded was K1 Class No. 62004 at Alnwick and J27 Class No. 65822 on North Blyth shed, both of which were seen on 26 September.

Back on the embankment south of Wivelsfield station on 1 October, I was to photograph Standard Class 4 tank No. 80085 on the 11.48 empty stock from Redhill to Brighton. At the time the movement of props, scenery etc., for the Royal Ballet was done by rail and on 11 October a 10.00 special was run from Bournemouth to Eastbourne via Worthing and Haywards Heath, hauled by Standard 5 No. 73018 to Haywards Heath, the onward journey being behind Crompton D6522. On 31 October I decided to go from Three Bridges to Groombridge via East Grinstead. At that time there were two stations at East Grinstead: the Low Level station, which in the present day joins the Northern Extension of the Bluebell Railway, and the High Level station, serving the trains from Three Bridges to Tunbridge Wells. By this time the majority of these services were DEMUs. After taking the staff at East Grinstead the train came to a stop to enable the guard to alight and remove a swan which had got onto the track. I have a feeling that this was a regular occurrence since the swan did not appear to be distressed. Such events were nothing unusual on country railways of course. There were complaints from passengers of the Polegate to Heathfield services of the train stopping between stations while the fireman shot a few rabbits; indeed, when my father was relief porter in that area we frequently had rabbits hanging in our outside coal shed. Having alighted at Groombridge, Standard Class 4 tank No. 80141 was seen on the 11.55 Tunbridge Wells West to Brighton via Uckfield. By the time I got to Birchden Junction, DEMU No. 1304 passed with the 11.58 Oxted to Brighton, followed by another Standard Class 4 tank, No. 80011, on the 11.56 Tonbridge to Eastbourne via Heathfield and Polegate. My final sighting on that misty day was at Eridge, where I spotted DEMU No. 1301 on the 12.41 Eastbourne to Tonbridge.

I was to take just a single non-industrial photograph in November, which was on 8 November, of rebuilt West Country No. 34026 *Yes Tor* leaving East Croydon on the reversible line with a football special from Norbury to Southampton. This was in connection with Crystal Palace FC's away match, which they won 0–1. Finally, on Boxing Day, I photographed the LBSCR Down station building at Burgess Hill. This was the last remaining part of the second station there and it was sadly knocked down by Network Rail a few years ago, just as a preservation order was being applied for.

8F No. 48129 passing Patricroft signal box with a freight working. 22 September 1964.

Jinty No. 47365 at Patricroft. 22 September 1964.

Jinty No. 47616 *Nobby* at Patricroft. 22 September 1964.

Class 4F No. 44468, complete with 'Not South of Crewe' yellow stripe, at Rose Grove shed. 22 September 1964.

8F No. 48281 at Rose Grove shed. 22 September 1964.

Horwich works shunter No. 11305 stored at Bolton shed after withdrawal. 22 September 1964.

Crab No. 42778 at Bolton. 22 September 1964.

Caprotti Class 5, fitted with a double chimney, seen leaving Newton Heath with a freight train. 23 September 1964.

Class 5 No. 44729 at Newton Heath. 23 September 1964.

Withdrawn Fowler Class 4 tank No. 42379 at Newton Heath. 23 September 1964.

Class 4F No. 44548 at Newton Heath. 23 September 1964.

Lancashire & Yorkshire Railway façade at Manchester Victoria station. 23 September 1964.

0F saddle tank No. 47001 at Barrow Hill. 24 September 1964.

Deeley 0F 0-4-0 tank No. 41528 at Barrow Hill. 24 September 1964.

WD 2-8-0 No. 90384 at Barrow Hill. 24 September 1964.

J27 Class No. 65822 at North Blyth shed. 26 September 1964.

Standard Class 4 tank No. 80085 passing Wivelsfield with the 11.48 empty stock from Redhill to Brighton. 1 October 1964.

Standard 5 No. 73018 approaching Keymer Junction with the 10.00 Royal Ballet special from Bournemouth to Eastbourne. 11 October 1964.

Standard 4 tank No. 80011 near Birchden Junction with the 11.56 Tonbridge to Eastbourne via Heathfield. 31 October 1964.

Rebuilt West Country Class No. 34026 *Yes Tor* on the reversible line, leaving East Croydon with a football special from Norbury to Southampton. 7 November 1964.

Former LBSCR Down platform buildings at Burgess Hill. 26 December 1964.

Chapter Three

1965 – A Busy Year and a Job Move Away from the Southern Region

Saturday 2 January was to be the last Saturday for steam working on the services between Redhill and Reading, although steam haulage of the inter-regional services was to continue. It was a sunny but cold day following an overnight frost and I walked the line from Deepdene to Gomshall, photographing as many of the services as possible, starting with U Class No. 31806 (now on the Watercress Line) with the 09.03 ex-Reading. The next service was the 09.45 ex-Reading, headed by another U Class, No. 31627. By the time I had reached Westcott, N class No. 31862 was seen on the 11.35 from Redhill, shortly followed in the reverse direction by another N, No. 31858, on the 11.05 from Reading. An interloper was Crompton D6589 with the 11.00 freight from Reading to Tonbridge. Near Gomshall, N Class No. 31816 passed on the 12.32 Reading to Redhill; finally U class No. 31627 was on the 13.35 ex-Redhill. The following day, 3 January, I was back at Redhill to photograph 'The Maunsell Commemorative' railtour run by the LCGB. Between Reading and Redhill N Class No. 31831 was used, replaced by another N, No. 31411, between Redhill and Tonbridge and Tonbridge to London Bridge via the Crowhurst Spur. Earlier on, Standard 4 tank No. 80068 worked the 14.11 Redhill to Tonbridge.

On 8 January I was back in the North East, visiting the collieries at Wearmouth, where Q6 No. 63437 was photographed, and Hylton, where another Q6 was photographed, this time No. 63387. I also visited Gateshead sheds, with Q6 No. 63444 and WD 2-8-0 No. 90723 being seen. Because of the times of day and film used all of the photographs were of a poor quality. The same quality problems existed the following day on a visit to Stirling where LMS Class 5 No. 45357 was unsuccessfully photographed on the 12.10 to Callander, although the photograph of another LMS Class 5, No. 45259, on the 11.30 ex-Edinburgh Waverley was much better. Also seen at Stirling was Britannia No. 70038 *Robin Hood* on the 12.20 Perth to Euston, Caprotti Standard 5 No. 73145 on a service to Glasgow, and Standard 4 2-6-0 No. 76046 on a freight train. A visit on the 10th to Dunfermline sheds revealed NBR J36 class No. 65288 fitted with a small snow plough and B1s Nos 61101 and 61072 on shed together with J37 No. 64623. Finally, at St Margaret's shed, J38 No. 65929, J36 No. 65234 on stationary boiler duties, B1 No. 61344 and a sad-looking No. 60007 *Sir Nigel Gresley* were seen. Overall, it was a poor photographic experience, with not the best film used for the lighting and weather conditions.

U Class No. 31806 at Deepdene with the 09.03 Reading to Redhill. 2 January 1965.

N Class No. 31858 near Westcott on the 11.00 Reading to Redhill. 2 January 1965.

U Class No. 31627 at Tangley with the 13.35 Redhill to Reading. 2 January 1965.

N Class No. 31411 leaving Redhill towards Tonbridge with the LCGB 'Maunsell Commemorative Railtour'. 3 January 1965.

Class 5 No. 45259 at Stirling with the 11.30 ex-Edinburgh Waverley. 9 January 1965.

Caprotti Standard
5 No. 73145 at
Stirling with a
Glasgow service.
9 January 1965.

Class J37 No. 65288 at Dunfermline shed, fitted with a snowplough. 10 January 1965.

Class J37 No. 65234 on stationary boiler duties at St Margaret's shed. 10 January 1965.

B1 Class No. 61344 at St Margaret's. 10 January 1965.

A4 Class No. 60007 *Sir Nigel Gresley* at St Margaret's shed. 10 January 1965.

I was able to make just a single main line visit in February. On a visit to industrial sites on 14 February a short visit was made to Kirkby-in-Ashfield shed to photograph LMS Class 4 2-6-0 No. 43010 and Class 4F 0-6-0s Nos 43918 and 44429. Then as now, weedkilling trains were run at intervals. On the Southern Region the stock was based at Horsham and consisted of a rake of old locomotive tenders. On an unknown date during March, N Class No. 31411 was photographed passing the allotments between Sanderstead and Selsdon on such a working. The weedkillers still run, albeit with tank wagons and a loco at each end. The N class has sadly been scrapped, but as far as I know, the array of allotments are still there. On 19 March I was to visit Imberhorne on what is now part of the Bluebell Railway's Northern Extension. North London Railway tank No. 2650 was being used on track removal duties, although it was not in steam on that date. Few photographs were taken in March, the final one being on the 28th, when I spotted Standard 5 No. 73022 passing through West Croydon with the Southern Counties Touring Society's 'The Southern Wanderer' railtour. This ran from Victoria to Horsham via Dorking and then down the Mid Sussex line to Southampton, Bournemouth Central and Blandford Forum to Templecombe, with No. 73022 working throughout. Return to Victoria was on the South Western main line behind Merchant Navy No. 35023 *Holland-Afrika Line*.

On 17 April I was in Scotland on industrial visits. Driving down south from Aberdeen, close to the main line we heard the distinctive sound of an A4 chime whistle. It was a matter of parking the vehicle, getting the camera out and trying for a snap shot of No. 60004 *William Whitelaw* heading the 11.48 milk train from Aberdeen to Perth.

LMS Class 4 2-6-0 No. 43010 at Kirkby-in-Ashfield shed. 14 February 1965.

Midland Class 4F No. 43918 at Kirkby-in-Ashfield. 14 February 1965.

N Class No. 31411 between Sanderstead and Selsdon with a weedkiller train, seen during March 1965.

North London tank No. 2650 awaiting track removal duties at Imberhorne. 19 March 1965.

Standard 5 No. 73022 near West Croydon with the Southern Counties Touring Society 'Southern Wanderer' railtour. 28 March 1965.

A4 No. 60004 *William Whitelaw* south of Aberdeen with the 11.48 milk train from Aberdeen to Perth. 17 April 1965.

On 1 May I was at Eastleigh after going to the Longmoor Military Railway open day. This proved to be my last visit there. Noted were West Countries Nos 34019 *Bideford*, 34033 *Chard* and 34041 *Wilton*, together with rebuilds Nos 34088 *213 Squadron* and 34097 *Holsworthy*. Also present was Merchant Navy Class No. 35003 *Royal Mail*. Awaiting restoration were Schools Class No. 30926 *Repton* and M7 No. 30053. In February 1967, these two were shipped to the USA, only to return in recent years. When making many of the visits we would either hire a car or, when I was Industrial Secretary for the LCGB, a minibus. I think we must have had a car for the Eastleigh visit since on the following day, 2 May, I went to the Bluebell Railway. On the way to Sheffield Park I called in to see the disused station at Newick & Chailey. The footbridge had gone prior to 1955, with the stairs down to the remaining platform and track going sometime between 1959 and 1960. The station building no longer exists, although Lower Station Road gives access to a housing estate. On the railway itself E4 Class 473 was the working locomotive, with others standing in the yard, including the petrol Howard shunter that had arrived during March. On the 29th I was at Guildford to photograph U Class No. 31800 departing with the 09.18 vans from Blisworth to Redhill and Class 2 tank No. 41301 on the 13.38 to Horsham via Baynards. Earlier in the day I was at Slinfold to witness the arrival of the 12.08 Horsham to Guildford, hauled by Class 2 tank No. 41297. The branch was to close to all traffic effective 12 June, with No. 41297 working the final passenger service. Another picturesque branch line closed following the Beeching philosophies. The return home was via Redhill sheds where N Class No. 31811 was present together with LMS Class 5 No. 44829, which had previously worked a pigeon special to Horsham.

West Country Class No. 34019 *Bideford* at Eastleigh shed. 1 May 1965.

West Country Class No. 34033 *Chard* at Eastleigh shed. 1 May 1965.

M7 Class No. 30053 awaiting restoration at Eastleigh. 1 May 1965.

Closed Newick &
Chailey station.
2 May 1965.

E4 Class No. 473 *Birch Grove* north of Sheffield Park with an Up train to Horsted Keynes.
2 May 1965.

LMS Class 2 tank No. 41301 leaving Guildford on the 13.38 to Horsham. 29 May 1965.

LMS Class 2 tank No. 41297 arriving at Slinfold with the 12.08 Guildford to Horsham. 29 May 1965.

N Class No. 31811 at Redhill shed. 29 May 1965.

LMS Class 5 No. 44829 at Redhill shed. 29 May 1965.

On 4 June a pigeon special was scheduled to be run from Newcastle to Hove. Whilst I worked in Engine Diagrams, I would not normally be involved in diagramming this particular service; however, since it scheduled to be a heavy load of some twenty coaches, I thought it wise to speak to my Motive Power colleagues across the corridor to get their views as what motive power they could arrange in view of the fact it was to run on a reasonably fast passenger schedule, intermingled with the regular electric passenger services and it would not be possible to fit it in with one of the existing Type 3 Crompton diagrams. As a result I telephoned my equivalent at Crewe and asked if they could schedule it a LMS Class 8F duty rather than a Class 5, to which they agreed. In the event the actual number of passenger bogies varied from the scheduled eighteen to twenty-one depending on which observer you spoke to; however, all agreed it was an impressive sight when passing through Clapham Junction and elsewhere. It was obvious that Willesden was also concerned about the load since on arriving at Latchmere Junction it was double-headed with Class 8 No. 48544 as the train engine and a Standard Class 2 2-6-0 as the pilot. The Southern crew said they did not need the pilot, which was sent back to Willesden. In any case, no problems were experienced during the trip south, which was a relief to me since if any had occurred my name would have been in lights. The return trip is a bit of a mystery. It was listed as going back the way it came; however, it was decreed the load was too heavy for the almost dead start incline from Hove to Preston Park and on to Haywards Heath and beyond, and new timings were published via the Steyning line, where a number of photographers had positioned themselves at various points only for no pigeon special to turn up. How and when the stock went back

LMS Class 8F No. 48544 leaving East Croydon with a pigeon special from Newcastle to Hove. 4 June 1965.

has not been established more than likely it was as an ad hoc working. As for No. 48544, it ran light engine from Hove to Redhill – by then the only Central section steam shed and itself scheduled to close that weekend – where it was noted over the weekend and later in Brighton station on 8 June, possibly to work the ad hoc return train. I was to photograph the special as it left East Croydon, passing the office I worked in at the time.

There were a number of scheduled passenger services and extras which were steam hauled, not just pigeon specials but a Car Sleeper train from Scotland initially to Eastbourne and latterly Newhaven. The main bulk of these were LMS or Standard Class 5 duties and, because of the timings and other activities I was involved in, did not attract the attention of my camera. As with most things in life there were always exceptions to the rule; one was on 19 June 1964 when Jubilee Class No. 45672 *Anson* arrived on the Car Sleeper. After being stabled overnight at Eastbourne, where servicing facilities were available, it was used to work a 18.45 return excursion to Romsey as far as Haywards Heath where West Country Class No. 34019 *Bideford* took over. However, on returning to Eastbourne No. 45672 became a failure and was deemed to be 'out of gauge' for the Central Section. I suspect this was more because Jubilees had never been part of the Route Availability book rather than having clearance issues. Eventually No. 45672 returned at some stage to Willesden. On the 21st yet another Jubilee, No. 45617 *Mauritius*, arrived at Newhaven and was impounded at Eastbourne, not returning light engine to Willesden until 30 July. Finally, on 26 June 1964, B1 No. 61313, a 41D Canklow engine, arrived at Lewes on a van train, probably a pigeon special, and on arrival at Eastbourne failed with a 'hot box'. It remained at Eastbourne until making its way to Redhill on 7 July and

Jubilee Class No. 45672 *Anson* leaving Eastbourne with the 18.45 return excursion to Romsey. 20 June 1964. (Photograph by S. C. Nash)

B1 Class No. 61313 at Easbourne. 26 June 1964. (Photograph by S. C. Nash)

V2 Class No. 60886 near Horbury with a train of coal wagons. 8 June 1965.

eventually returned north sometime after 16 July. While the events surrounding No. 48544 were happening I was in Cumbria on an industrial visit, returning via Horbury, where on the 8th V2 Class No. 60886 was seen working a train of coal wagons.

I was just to take one series of BR steam photographs in July. This was on the 3rd, when I was persuaded to help on the LCGB (Bedford Branch) 'Northamptonshire Branches Brake Van Tour', hauled by Standard Class 2 No. 78038. My function was unclear but seemed to be to ensure passengers got on and off the brake vans safely; for this I was given a free ride. The tour started from Wellingborough Midland Road, running to Higham Ferrers and back and onto Wellingborough London Road. From there we visited Northampton Castle, Cransley, Loddington, Twywell and Cranford before finishing at Kettering. No. 78038 disgraced itself by stalling between Kettering and Loddington and having to set back some way to have a second and successful attempt. These branch lines served some of the ironstone quarries; these were all shortly to close as being either exhausted or uneconomic with the branch lines themselves eventually following.

August was far from a productive photographic month. I made a visit one day to the Isle of Wight where W20 *Shanklin* and W30 *Shorwell* were on shed at Ryde St Johns, while W21 *Sandown* and W27 *Merstone* appeared to be stored. A working loco was W18 *Ningwood*. I also visited Smallbrook Junction, where several unsuccessful photographs were taken.

It was about this time that I felt my career at Essex House had stagnated and was applying for positions elsewhere. One such application was in Leeds with the BRB Timetable Development Group, and this was rewarded with a series of aptitude tests and an interview. Returning to Essex House I thought I would bide my time and see what

BR Standard
Class No. 78038
restarting the LCGB
'Northamptonshire
Branches Brakevan
Tour' after
stalling between
Wellingborough
and Loddington.
The person holding
his liquid lunch is
Malcolm Burton, prime
organiser of many of
the LCGB railtours at
that time! 3 July 1965.

LSWR O2 Class W18 *Ningwood* leaving Ryde St Johns during August 1965.

happened, and as luck would have it was appointed to another position, which in the event I did not actually take up. However, pending the actual start-up I went to a training course on one of the possible techniques it would be likely I would be required to use. On that course one of the presenters, who I had met in Leeds, approached me to congratulate me, saying I would be joining his team in Leeds the following Monday. I explained that this was news to me and I had not been told and neither had Essex House Staff Office. This of course meant I was never to return to Essex House. In fact, when meeting a former colleague a few years ago he said they were all mystified since it appeared I had disappeared and no one knew where to! On arriving at Leeds at the appointed hour we found that, except for the Scottish Region, the new team members had been selected on a regional basis: one from Liverpool Street, one from Paddington, one from Leeds, myself from the Southern Region, and the member for the Midland Region had been the stationmaster at Mytholmroyd. The management team itself had originated from the North Eastern Region at York. We found that our task was to develop a computer-based application to provide flexible on-demand timetables for freight movements – in fact, the genesis of the later 'merry-go-round' operations for the Yorkshire power stations and collieries. We went through an intensive training period in the computer programming and mathematical techniques required before starting the serious work.

Since I was returning to Sussex each weekend, certainly for the initial period prior to permanent accommodation could be arranged, I did not have my cameras and therefore no photographs were taken. I was at home on 3 October when the LCGB 'Vectis Farewell' railtour was run from Waterloo to Portsmouth Harbour via Horsham, hauled

West Country Class No. 34002 *Salisbury* between Itchingfield Junction and Arundel with the LCGB 'Vectis Farewell' railtour. 3 October 1965. (Photograph by David Hill)

by West Country Class No. 34002 *Salisbury* and I wrote, more in hope than expectation, to Harold Roberts, the Divisional Movements Manager at Essex House (who had previously arranged for my ride in the cab of one of the Southern electric locomotives), asking whether it would be possible for a cab pass on No. 34002 between Horsham and Portsmouth. To my surprise, this duly arrived and I joined the crew and inspector at Horsham, displacing an unhappy individual who was already on the footplate and had to continue his journey 'on the cushions'. I knew the inspector from my days in Engine Diagrams and had met the driver on a couple of previous occasions as well. The railtour itself stopped at Chichester and a pair of Q1s took over for the short trips to Lavant and return, although I stayed with No. 34002, not leaving the footplate until arrival at Portsmouth Harbour.

Our office at Leeds was situated in a new office block over City station. All the testing of our programs was undertaken at the computer centre at Stooperdale offices in Darlington, and required one or more of us to make frequent visits there. There happened to be a weekday service from Leeds to Darlington via Harrogate, and since this was steam-hauled, usually by A1 Class No. 60124 *Kenilworth*, it became to the usual choice of travel. One cold November day I was to visit Darlington sheds to capture No. 60124 together with K1s Nos 62041 and 62048, as well as J27 No. 65859. On another November day I went to York sheds to photograph B1 Class No. 61319 and WD 2-8-0 No. 90518. Of interest inside the shed was a Jinty 0-6-0T, which had been recently stripped down and converted to mobile steam-heating boiler No. 2022. The weekends in Leeds seemed to be pretty gloomy affairs; however, I was able to visit Engine Shed Junction at Holbeck and see what workings there were about. Many of these local freights were hauled by Standard Class 3 2-6-0s, more than likely either No. 77001, No. 77003 or No. 77010. Also seen were LMS Class 8Fs, including No. 48721. However, the conditions were not conducive to photography and I tended not to stay there very long.

A1 Class No. 60124 *Kenilworth* on Darlington shed during November 1965.

K1 Class No. 62048 at Darlington shed during November 1965.

J27 Class No. 65859 at Darlington shed during November 1965.

B1 Class No. 61319
at York shed during
November 1965.

WD 2-8-0 No. 90518
at York shed during
November 1965.

A BR Standard Class 3,
either No. 77001,
No. 77003 or No. 77010,
emerging from the murk on
a freight working at Engine
Shed Junction during
November 1965.

Chapter Four

1966 – A Final Year of Photography

I did not take many railway photographs in the first two months of 1966, save for a single visit in February to a still miserable Engine Shed Junction. Perhaps that was a feature of that part of Leeds. Anyway just the one photograph resulted, of LMS Class 4 2-6-0 No. 43135 on a mineral train. On 12 March I went on an industrial visit organised by the North West Branch of The LCGB, and as part of that we visited Bolton Shed where the only locomotive note was the derailed Stanier Class 4 tank No. 42663.

Following advice from some of my work colleagues, I decided to visit the Sowerby Bridge area on 19 March. Sightings of note were LMS Class 5 No. 44936 on a freight heading for Rose Grove, LMS Class 8Fs Nos 48340 and 48547 also on eastbound freights and Jubilee Class No. 45647 *Sturdee* on the 12.05 football special from Leeds to Blackburn, a game which Leeds United won 2–3.

LMS Class 4 2-6-0 No. 43135 at Engine Shed Junction on a freight working during February 1966.

Stanier Class 4 tank No. 42663 derailed at Bolton shed. 16 March 1966.

LMS Class 5 No. 44936 near Sowerby Bridge with a freight to Rose Grove. 19 March 1966.

LMS 8F No. 48340 near Sowerby Bridge with a freight working. 19 March 1966.

LMS 8F No. 48547 near Sowerby Bridge with a freight working. 19 March 1966.

Jubilee Class No. 45647 *Sturdee* near Sowerby Bridge with the 12.05 football special from Leeds to Blackburn. 19 March 1966.

On 29 April a visit was made to Huddersfield, where 8F No. 48182 was seen working a freight to Healey Mills and Jubilee Class No. 45627 *Sierra Leone* was on the 17.27 Manchester to York. The following day I was at Skipton, where most of my photographs were far from successful. However, Jubilee No. 45593 *Kolhapur* was seen on the Jubilee Society 'South Yorkshire No. 5 Railtour', which ran from Bradford to Carnforth, Carlisle and return. No. 45593 failed at Carlisle and had to be replaced by Britannia Class No. 70034. 'Peak' Diesel Electric D66 was seen working the 1X16 Huddersfield to Carlisle, while Class 5 No. 44828 worked the 08.14 Heysham to Leeds. Meanwhile, in the sidings were Jinty No. 47417 and the stored LMS Class 2 tank No. 41243.

The London branch of the LCGB arranged a visit to LTE Neasden where former GWR 5700 Class pannier tanks L93 (ex-GWR No. 7779) and L95 (ex-GWR No. 5764) were present. Metrovick Bo-Bo electric loco No. 1 *John Lyons* was also there. There was always one of the electric locos lurking at Aldgate East station between duties, I can recall seeing the preserved loco No. 12 *Sarah Siddons* passing the former Pullman works at Preston Park on 15 July 1983 prior to an open day at Lovers Walk and Brighton Station the following day. Although, as we know, railtours were not my thing, I was tempted by a free ticket to help on the LCGB/*Railway Magazine* 'Picardy and Somme Railtour' that ran on 15 May. This originated at Victoria when EDL – Class 73 in today's terminology – E6029 and electric loco E5005 'topped and tailed' the special working to Folkestone Harbour and return. After crossing the Channel the party was split in two and I joined the first special to Longeau, which was hauled by ex-PLM Pacific No. 231C22. The second special was hauled by an 141R. After a visit to Longeau sheds, where several 141Rs were

LMS Class 2MT 2-6-2T No. 41241 stored at Skipton. 30 April 1966.

Ex-GWR 5700 Class pannier tank L95 at Neasden. 7 June 1966.

LTE Metrovick Bo-Bo Electric No. 1 *John Lyons* at Neasden. 7 June 1966.

present as well at an 030T 0-6-0 tank, an ex-USATC loco similar to the USA tanks on the Southern Region; two magnificent 150P 2-10-0s, one being No. 150P145; Pacific No. 231E3, which was originally scheduled to work one of the special trains but had failed and was promptly withdrawn; No. 230D125, a 4-6-0 locomotive; and 0-10-0 tank No. 050TE18. Having then, as now, no knowledge of Continental railways, these types were a mystery to me. The return special I was on was worked by No. 141R334, and the other was worked by No. 141R476. It was an interesting day out and well worth the trip.

I think I must have been on holiday at the time, since several days were spent at the end of the month visiting a number of industrial sites in the North East. This could well have been the time when one of the small group who usually accompanied us on such trips, a top link passed fireman at King's Cross Top Shed, said to me that if I caught a certain service north from King's Cross he would arrange a way for me just prior to departure to get into the cab of the Deltic so that I would be up front for the non-stop run to Durham. Pure magic! The only British Railways photograph taken on that weekend was on 31 May of 9F 'Spaceship' No. 92097 crossing Anfield Plain with a coal train to Consett. We

SNCF Pacific No. 231C22 waiting to depart from Dieppe to Longeau with the LCGB 'Picardy and Somme Railtour'. 15 May 1966.

SNCF No. 141R476 waiting depart from Longeau for Dieppe with a return portion of the LCGB 'Picardy and Somme Railtour'. 15 May 1966.

Class 9F No. 92096 crossing Anfield Plain with a coal train to Consett. 31 May 1966.

were not sure of the time it was due, so we stood waiting in the field with a collection of bovine friends!

One of my bosses at Leeds was J. Brian Hollingsworth, who later had a narrow gauge railway in his garden at Tan-y-Bwlch, and just before leaving work on 3 June, he asked if I would like to accompany him, his wife and an American friend on a trip to Copy Pit. Although at the time Copy Pit meant nothing to me, I was only too pleased to accept his offer. All I had to do was to be at Hebden Bridge to meet up with them. So, on the 4th I was at Hebden Bridge to photograph Jubilee Class No. 45647 *Sturdee* departing on the 08.30 Leeds to Blackpool prior to travelling, complete with a picnic lunch and homemade ginger beer, to Copy Pit. At Copy Pit we were to meet up with several railway photographers, including A. E. 'Dusty' Durrant, who was to write a major book about Beyer-Garratt locomotives. At Copy Pit itself we saw a number of LMS Class 5 locos on mainly special workings, including Nos 45080, 45209 on what could have been a regular service, and 45428 on 1X38. Also seen were LMS Class 8F banking 1X43 and WD 2-8-0 No. 902333 drifting past on a freight train. After finishing at Copy Pit we visited Carnforth shed, and then went on to the Carlisle and Settle line to observe the LCGB 'Fellsman' railtour.

Jubilee Class No. 45647 *Sturdee* leaving Hebden Bridge with the 08.30 Leeds to Blackpool. 4 June 1966.

LMS Class 5 No. 45090 at Copy Pit with an excursion train. 4 June 1966.

WD Class 2-8-0 No. 90233 at Copy Pit with a freight service. 4 June 1966.

LMS 8F No. 48435 at Copy Pit, banking the 1X43. 4 June 1966.

LMS Class 5 No. 45428 working excursion 1X38 at Copy Pit. 4 June 1966.

Britannia Class No. 70032 *Tennyson* at Farnley. 5 June 1966.

Class 9F No. 92075 on a freight working near Settle. 30 July 1966.

An LMS Class 5 leaving Penrith for Carlisle. 30 July 1966.

One shed that I was to visit a number of times was Farnley, where, on 5 June, Britannia Class No. 70032, the former *Tennyson*, was seen waiting to work back to Crewe. Another visit to Farnley on 17 July found Black 5 No. 44729.

30 June was a sunny day in London where England were to win the football World Cup; however, it was not so at Carlisle, where it was wet and miserable. On my way there I saw Jubilee Class No. 45593 *Kolhapur* at Settle on the 1S52, while 9F No. 92075 was photographed on a freight service. My journey to Carlisle was behind a Class 5, which I photographed from the train leaving Penrith. The weather at Carlisle was pretty miserable, but seen arriving was Britannia No. 70002 *Geoffrey Chaucer* with the 12.37 Manchester to Glasgow, followed by Jubilee Class No. 45675 *Hardy* with the 09.15 St Pancras to Glasgow. Additionally, a quartet of Black Fives were in a line awaiting their next duties: No. 45025 on 1M32; No. 45033 on 1M52; No. 44829 on 1M38; and No. 44892 on a freight. LMS Class 2 tank No. 41222 was acting as the station pilot.

On 19 August I called at Carnforth on the way to Shap and saw LMS Class 5 No. 44878 pass through with an Up freight train. Our visit to Shap the following day was a bit of a disaster; having stopped overnight in Kendal, we contrived to miss the bus and arrived at Shap too late for most of the steam workings. However, Brush Type 4 diesel was D1616 was seen on the Up Royal Scot, as well as English Electric Type 4 D269 on the 10.25 Edinburgh to Birmingham. Steam workings included LMS Class 5s Nos 44899 and 45296 on freight trains, Ivatt Class 4MT No. 43039 with just a brake van

Jubilee Class No. 45675 *Hardy* at Carlisle with the 09.15 St Pancras to Glasgow. 30 July 1966.

LMS Class 2T No. 41222 as the Carlisle station pilot. 30 July 1966.

LMS Class 5s No. 45025 is seen waiting to work 1M32 while No. 45033 is waiting to work 1M52, No. 44829 is waiting to work 1M38 and No. 44892 is on a freight train. 30 July 1966.

LMS Class 4 2-6-0 No. 43039 at Shap with a brake van. 20 August 1966.

LNWR lamp at Shap station. 20 August 1966.

and 8F No. 48356 on an Up freight. By now the station closure notices had been put up; I wonder what happened to the rather fine station lamps?

On 3 September I was to visit Mirfield and other places in that area. At Mirfield LMS Class 5 No. 44824 worked an eastbound freight, while other freight workings were headed by 8Fs Nos 48152 and 48547. No. 48152 was seen again on another freight, this time at Huddersfield. Going on to Hillhouse, Jubilee No. 45562 *Alberta* was on the 09.08 Leeds to Poole, Class 8F No. 48269 worked the 09.06 Bradford to Poole and WD 2-8-0 No. 90649 was on a short freight train. Finally, at Heaton Lodge 8F No. 48159 worked a freight service, as did WD 2-8-0 No. 90698. B1 No. 61237 was on a short parcels train, and LMS Class No. 45080 headed the 09.20 Scarborough to Manchester. My final visit in September was on the 23rd to Farnley, where I was to photograph resident Jubilee Class No. 45562 *Alberta*, complete with its neat hand-painted name, the original plates having been removed. These were to prove to be the last British Railways steam photographs I would take since the testing of the routine I had been developing was transferred to the computers at English Electric, Kidsgrove and Nottingham University, and as a result I relocated to an office at Derby station.

LMS Class 5 No. 44824 near Mirfield with a freight train. 3 September 1966.

LMS 8F No. 48152 passing Mirfield shed with a freight train. 3 September 1966.

LMS 8F No. 48547 near Mirfield with a freight service. 3 September 1966.

LMS 8F No. 48152 near Huddersfield with a freight service. 3 September 1966.

LMS 8F No. 48269 near Hillhouse on the 09.08 Bradford to Poole. 3 September 1966.

WD 2-8-0 No. 90649 near Hillhouse with a short freight. 3 September 1966.

WD 2-8-0 No. 90698 near Heaton Lodge with a freight train. 3 September 1966.

B1 Class No. 61237 on a parcels train near Heaton Lodge. 3 September 1966.

LMS Class 5 No. 45080 near Heaton Lodge with the 09.20 Scarborough to Manchester. 3 September 1966.

Jubilee Class No. 45562 *Alberta* at Farnley.
23 September 1966.

The painted name on Jubilee Class No. 45562 *Alberta*. 23 September 1966.

What Happened Next

The transfer of my job to Derby meant moving all my belongings, including cameras, back to my family home in Sussex. In addition, I was now in weekday-only accommodation, which meant that opportunities to make photographic trips were restricted. The use of steam, my prime reason for railway photographs, was by now restricted to the north-western parts of England, plus the remaining Waterloo to Weymouth services prior to the completion of the electrification of that route, and I more or less stopped taking railway photographs as diesel and electric locomotives and multiple units were of little or no interest to me. In early 1967 I moved to a new position at Marylebone, where I worked on computer program standards, and finally in September I was to leave railway employment altogether and work in the private sector. I had found my short stay very interesting, not only for the photographic opportunities but because it was the first time I had come close to some of the politics in railway operations. As a group we had close contact with the Transport Ministry, at that time headed by Barbara Castle, and our manager frequently told us how frustrated she became at times with her fellow cabinet members when trying to get progress on finance for forward-thinking ideas, being defeated many times by the 'Roads' lobby. And, of course, it was at a time when the iron and steel industries were being nationalised. To compound the problem, there was a series of industrial disputes to contend with. I think some of the problems in rail operations at that time are best described in Gerard Fiennes's book *I Tried to Run a Railway*.

Since 1967 I have taken the odd railway photograph, mainly on heritage railways. However, where I now live there are only so many photographs I can take of Class 313, 377, 385 and 700 electric units, and the occasional Class 66 'shed', without a severe case of déjà vu occurring.

Sources and Dedication

This book is dedicated to the late Chris Gammell, who suggested I digitise my images; to Malcolm Burton of the LCGB who organised many of the trips I went on; to Harold Roberts, Divional Movements Manager at Essex House and later Chaiman of the Bluebell Railway; and finally to J. Brian Hollingsworth for inviting me to accompany him to Copy Pit.

Except where indicated, all of the photographs were taken by myself and in the main have not been published before. A Montana TLR roll film camera and a Reflexa SLR 35 mm camera were the cameras used with a variety of monochrome, colour roll and transparency films.

Reference has been made to the following publications:

Black Eight (issue 130).
Longworth, Hugh, *British Railways Steam Locomotives 1948–1969* (OPC, 2010).
Steam Days No. 256 (December 2010).
Various Ian Allan *ABCs*
Verrall, Charlie, *Search for Steam: British Railways 1951–1962* (Amberley, 2018).
Verrall, Charlie, *Steam around Basingstoke and Salisbury* (Amberley, 2017).

Reference has also been made to the files at www.sixbellsjunction.co.uk for details of various railtours seen.

Thanks go to all the railway workers who never queried why I was on the lineside taking photographs or in different steam sheds with or without a permit. Thanks also to my co-workers at Essex House and Leeds for their encouragement – especially those at Leeds who suggested places to visit, took me into their homes for real Yorkshire pudding and introduced me to the original, and best, Harry Ramsden's Fish and Chippery.

Many thanks go to Brian Read, who once again took on the task of checking the original draft document. As usual his help was invaluable. Thanks also Mick Hymans for researching his collection of *Railway Observers* in response to my queries. Mention needs to be made of the help from various members of the Bluebell Railway archive team for allowing me to dig into their boxes and boxes of material to resolve a number of Southern Region timetable queries. Thanks to Bill Jones from Brighton MPD who took me on the short ride on the cab of No. 34066 from Brighton Station to the Top

Yard turntable – a short trip but very different – and Dave Rollins from King's Cross Top Shed for smuggling into the cab of a Deltic for a non-stop ride to Durham. Thanks also to Keith Long, who unbeknown to me was working in the signal box at Engine Shed Junction at the time I was based in Leeds and has subsequently provided information relating to the local workings there.

Thanks also to the good people at Amberley Publishing for their encouragement and help with this tome.

Finally, thanks have to go to my long-suffering wife Gillian, who knew little about the fascination of steam railways until our honeymoon, when she was subject to visits to some of the Little Railways of Wales; also to my youngest son, Jeremy, who undertook the task of checking the printers' proofs.

And last but not least, thanks to you the reader for getting this far.